OIL

OIL

OIL

FLOUR

FLOUR

FLOUR

Kimmel, Eric A.

The runaway tortilla / by Eric A. Kimmel ; illustrated by Randy Cecil.

First Edition

p.   cm.

Summary: In this Southwestern version of the Gingerbread Man, a tortilla runs away from the woman who is about to cook him.

ISBN: 1-890817-18-X

[1. Fairy tales. 2. Folklore.]

I. Cecil, Randy, ill. II. Gingerbread boy. English. III. Title.

PZ8.K527 Ru   2000

398.2'0979'01-dc21

[E]00-020487

All rights reserved

Library of Congress catalog card number: [E]00-020487

Creative Director: Bretton Clark

Designed by: Billy Kelly

Editor: Margery Cuyler

Printed in Belgium

This book has a trade reinforced binding.

For games, links and more, visit our interactive Web site:

www.winslowpress.com

The Runaway Tortilla

To Sancho

E.A.K.

For Bebe, Celina, and Toots

R.C.

The Runaway Tortilla

by **Eric A. Kimmel**

illustrated by **Randy Cecil**

WINSLOW PRESS

DELRAY BEACH, FLORIDA • NEW YORK

O nce upon a time in Texas, down by the Rio Grande, there lived a couple known to all as Tía Lupe and Tío José. Tía Lupe and Tío José owned a taquería called El Papagayo Feliz, The Happy Parrot. Cowboys came from near and far to eat there. Everyone said that Tía Lupe and Tío José made the best enchiladas, burritos, tacos, and fajitas in all of Texas.

The secret was the tortillas. Tía Lupe made each one by hand. They were as light as a cloud and as soft as the fuzz on a baby's cheek. "Tía Lupe," the cowboys warned, "you better not make these tortillas any lighter. Some day they'll up and run away!"

"Don't worry. That will never happen," laughed Tío José.

No sooner had he spoken when a tortilla jumped up and cried, "Oh yes it will! I'm too beautiful to eat!"

"I'm sorry, tortilla," said Tía Lupe. "All tortillas are made to be eaten. That is what they are for."

"You'll have to catch me first!" the tortilla exclaimed. She leaped from the griddle and rolled out the door before anyone could catch her. Tía Lupe and Tío José chased after the tortilla, running as fast as they could.

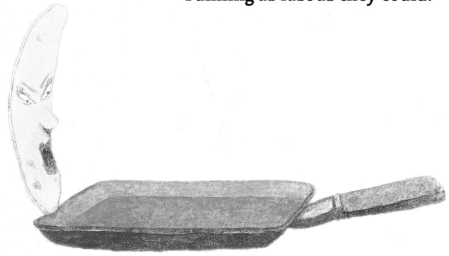

Through the streets and out of town rolled the tortilla. She rolled into the desert, where nothing grows but mesquite and cactus. Along the way she passed two horned toads basking on a rock.

"Come bask with us, Señorita Tortilla!" the horned toads said.

"Lazy lizards, catch me if you can!" the tortilla laughed.

Run as fast as fast can be. You won't get a bite of me. Doesn't matter what you do. I'll be far ahead of you!

And away she rolled, with two horned toads scampering and Tía Lupe and Tío José running after her, as fast as they could go.

Down the hill and past the cutbank rolled the tortilla. She passed three donkeys braying.

"Hee-haw! Hee-haw! Come bray with us, Señorita Tortilla!"

"Silly jackasses! Catch me if you can!" the tortilla yelled.

Run as fast as fast can be. You won't get a bite of me. Doesn't matter what you do. I'll be far ahead of you!

And away she rolled, with three donkeys trotting, two horned toads scampering, and Tía Lupe and Tío José running after her, as fast as they could go.

Across the highway and over the bridge rolled the tortilla.
She passed four jackrabbits leaping over a mesquite bush.
"Come leap with us, Señorita Tortilla!" said the jackrabbits.
"Foolish bunnies! Catch me if you can!" the tortilla yelled.

Run as fast as fast can be. You won't get a bite of me. Doesn't matter what you do. I'll be far ahead of you!

And away she rolled, with four jackrabbits leaping, three donkeys trotting, two horned toads scampering, and Tía Lupe and Tío José running after her, as fast as they could go.

Around a wrecked car and through an old tire rolled the tortilla. She passed five rattlesnakes shaking their rattles.

"Come make music with us, Señorita Tortilla," the rattlesnakes hissed.

"Rowdy rattlers! Catch me if you can!" the tortilla yelled.

Run as fast as fast can be. You won't get a bite of me.

Doesn't matter what you do. I'll be far ahead of you!

And away she rolled, with five rattlesnakes slithering, four jackrabbits leaping, three donkeys trotting, two horned toads scampering, and Tía Lupe and Tío José running after her, as fast as they could go.

Out and in and in and out of a box canyon rolled the tortilla. She passed six bold buckaroos, loping along on their pinto ponies.

"Come ride with us, Señorita Tortilla," the buckaroos cried.

"Crazy cowboys! Catch me if you can!" the tortilla yelled.

Run as fast as fast can be.   You won't get a bite of me.

And away she rolled, with six buckaroos galloping, five rattlesnakes slithering, four jackrabbits leaping, three donkeys trotting, two horned toads scampering, and Tía Lupe and Tío José running after her, as fast as they could go.

Suddenly she stopped. Up ahead, at the edge of an arroyo, she saw Señor Coyote. He sat on the sand with his mouth open.

"Help me, Señorita Tortilla!" he moaned.

"What is the matter?" the tortilla asked.

Señor Coyote answered, "I was standing here by the arroyo with my mouth open when a grasshopper jumped in. He is caught in my throat. I cough and cough, but I cannot get him out. Will you help me, Tortilla? Will you go down into my throat and pull out that wicked grasshopper?"

"Not I! How stupid do you think I am?" the tortilla answered. "I don't trust coyotes. I don't trust anyone."

Señor Coyote opened his mouth wider. "You don't have to be afraid of me, little tortilla. I can't hurt you. I'm not even hungry. Won't you help me? Please!"

"What will you give me if I do?" the tortilla said.

"Oh, Señorita Tortilla," Señor Coyote whispered. "I know where a great treasure is buried. I will take you there and share it with you if you pull this grasshopper from my throat."

"Show me the treasure," the tortilla said.

"Take out the grasshopper," Señor Coyote replied.

The tortilla rolled into Señor Coyote's mouth. She looked around. "Where is this grasshopper? I don't see him."

"Go deeper!"

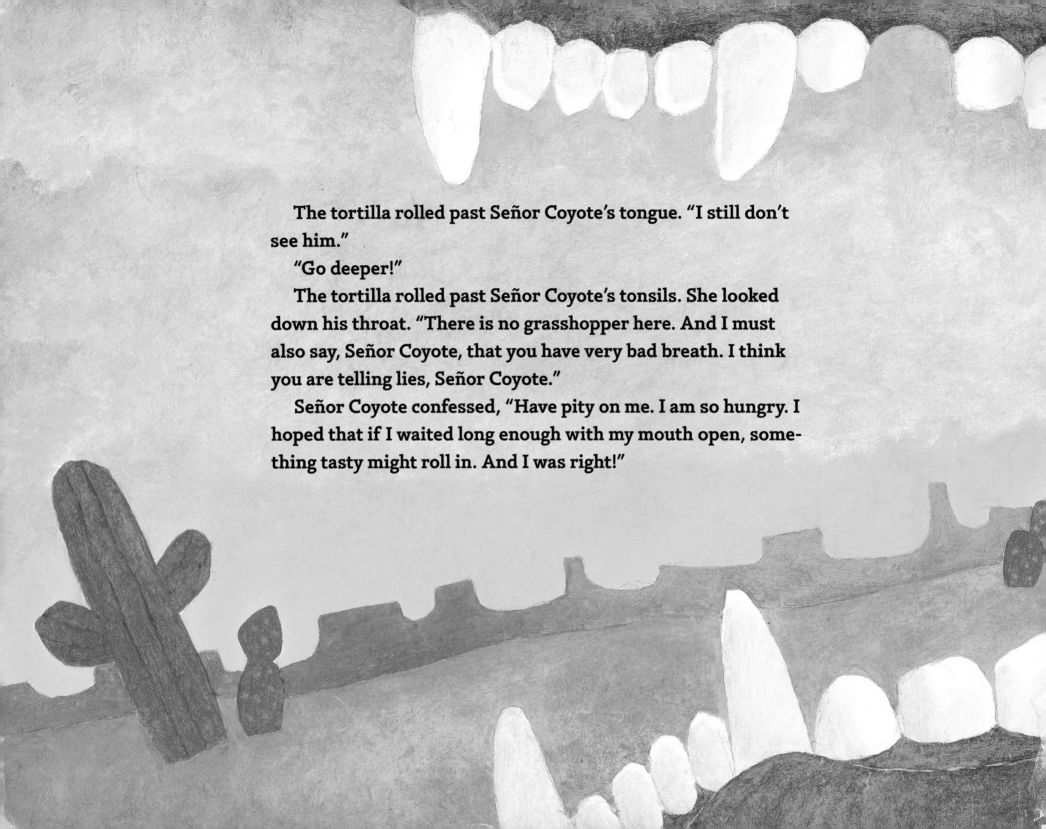

The tortilla rolled past Señor Coyote's tongue. "I still don't see him."

"Go deeper!"

The tortilla rolled past Señor Coyote's tonsils. She looked down his throat. "There is no grasshopper here. And I must also say, Señor Coyote, that you have very bad breath. I think you are telling lies, Señor Coyote."

Señor Coyote confessed, "Have pity on me. I am so hungry. I hoped that if I waited long enough with my mouth open, something tasty might roll in. And I was right!"

That was the end of the tortilla.
And that is the end of the story.
As for the treasure, it's still waiting
for someone to find it.
So all that's left is the song.

Run as fast as fast can be. You won't get a bite of me. Doesn't matter what you do. I'll be far ahead of you!